A History of Thessaly: From the Earliest Historical Times to the Accession of Philip V. of Macedonia

Roland Grubb Kent

A HISTORY OF THESSALY

FROM THE

EARLIEST HISTORICAL TIMES

TO THE

ACCESSION OF PHILIP V. OF MACEDONIA

PRINTED IN PART

THESIS

PRESENTED TO THE FACULTY OF THE DEPARTMENT OF PHILOSOPHY OF THE
UNIVERSITY OF PENNSYLVANIA, IN PARTIAL FULFILMENT OF THE
REQUIREMENTS FOR THE DEGREE OF DOCTOR OF PHILOSOPHY

BY

ROLAND GRUBB KENT

PRESS OF
THE NEW ERA PRINTING COMPANY,
LANCASTER, PA.
1904

PREFACE.

The history of Thessaly may at present be found stowed away in the larger and more detailed histories of Greece ; monographs on particular features or events exist in the periodicals, and some meager encyclopaedia articles are also at hand ; but in such form the material is too inaccessible to give more than a general vague idea. To present this therefore in connected form is the purpose of this dissertation ; and if a little light is occasionally thrown upon some point formerly obscure, the writer will be more than satisfied.

In doing this an attempt has been made to work up the subject chiefly from ancient sources ; hence the references to the works of modern writers may seem disproportionately few. This should not be taken to mean however that recent literature on the subject has been neglected ; for that would be untrue. Among many helpful works and shorter articles the writer wishes to acknowledge especial indebtedness to Busolt's "Griechische Geschichte," Schäfer's "Demosthenes und seine Zeit" and Droysen's "Geschichte des Hellenismus," which have served as correctives to many an error. And he will farther feel truly grateful to any reader, who, detecting the errors that doubtless still remain, will take the trouble to inform him of them.

In quoting authorities, so far as possible the comma is used to separate references to the same work or to the same author, and the semicolon to separate references to different authors. The exigencies of the case have in a few instances caused variations from this general practice. For convenience, spurious works (as for example many of the orations of Demosthenes) are in the references assigned without comment to the author with whose name they are commonly though wrongly connected.

A confession of faith seems necessary nowadays upon the subject of the spelling of proper names. The plan here adopted is

iii

to give them in their Latin forms; but for various reasons the following modifications of this principle are made : (1) The final ν of names ending in $\omega\nu$ is retained, as Menon. (2) For distinction from ϵ and ι, $\epsilon\iota$ is transliterated by ê or î, as Chaeronêa, Sperchîus; and to avoid confusion with final $o\varsigma$, final $ov\varsigma$ is expressed by ûs, as Rhamnûs. (3) Heracles, Hecabe and similar forms are retained, where the Latin varies decidedly from the Greek. (4) A few names such as Aristotle, Plato and Pindar, and of course Athens, Corinth and Thebes, are retained in the forms familiar in English.

For constant assistance and encouragement and helpful suggestion, the writer desires to express his heartfelt thanks to Professor W. A. Lamberton, of this University.

ROLAND G. KENT.

UNIVERSITY OF PENNSYLVANIA,
PHILADELPHIA, PA., March 1, 1903.

On account of the length of this dissertation, only Chapter V and Appendixes I and II have been printed. As these portions contain nearly all of the investigations giving new results, permission to leave the remainder unprinted has been granted by the Executive Committee of the Department of Philosophy.

January 28, 1904.

CONTENTS.

CHAPTER VII. PHILIP AND ALEXANDER.

CHAPTER VIII. THESSALY UNDER THE SUCCESSORS OF
ALEXANDER.

APPENDIX I. THE RULING FAMILIES OF PHARSALUS.

APPENDIX II. THE RELATIONS BETWEEN THESSALY AND ATHENS.

APPENDIX III. THE HIGHEST THESSALIAN MAGISTRACY.

APPENDIX IV. THE EXPEDITION OF CYRUS.

APPENDIX V. ALEXANDER'S CONQUEST OF ASIA.

APPENDIX VI. CINEAS, MINISTER OF PYRRHUS.

CHAPTER V.

FROM THE PERSIAN WARS TO LYCOPHRON OF PHERAE.

§1. At the beginning of the Persian War the Greeks had vowed to dedicate to the god at Delphi a tenth of the possessions of all those Greeks who under no compulsion submitted to the barbarian.[1] Therefore an army commanded by Leotychidas king of Sparta was after the close of the war sent to Thessaly to punish the Aleuadae for their attitude. It was transported by sea to Pagasae, where the fleet remained while the army invaded the interior of the country. By this means the difficult passage of the mountains of Phthiotis was avoided. The Thessalian generals Aristomedes and Angelus were defeated in battle, and all promised a speedy success for the Lacedaemonians, when the Aleuads shrewdly bribed Leotychidas, and he withdrew to the coast. Even before he had left the country his dishonesty became evident, for he was found to be in possession of wealth for which he could not account. He was taken back to Sparta, where he was condemned to death, a sentence whose execution he escaped by fleeing for refuge to the temple of Athena Alea at Tegea.[2]

At the spring Pylaea, presumably of the same year, the Lacedaemonians desired to exclude from the Amphictyony the nations that did not take up arms against the invaders; the issue was raised especially in regard to the Thessalians, the Thebans and the Argives. But the Athenians, led by Themistocles, their hieromnemon at the time, opposed the move, for they saw that action would then be confined to a few cities among which Sparta would easily take the leading position, while Athens would take a minor place. The Athenian influence was strong enough to defeat the proposition.[3]

§1. 1. Herod. VII 132.
§1. 2. Herod. VI 72; Paus. III 7 9 sq.; Plut. Them. 20, Mor. 859 D.
§1. 3. Plut. Them. 20.

1

The date of these events is uncertain. Grote[4] places them in 478 or 477, as the punishment of the Aleuads would be only the natural continuation of the war against the Persian; but there are certain difficulties with this dating. Leotychidas ascended the throne in 491, and ruled twenty-two years,[5] according to Diodorus.[6] This would put his exile, and consequently the Thessalian campaign, in 470/69. Further, Archidamus, his grandson and successor, who died between June 428 and the spring of 426, is said to have reigned forty-two years,[7] which agrees with the previous statement. On the other hand, Themistocles is said by Plutarch to have had the intention of setting on fire the Greek fleet as it lay at Pagasae, to insure the naval supremacy of Athens.[8] In this passage the fleet is represented as stationed at Pagasae during the winter after the battle of Plataea, that is, of 479/8. At any rate, the campaign and the proposed exclusion of the Thessalians from the Amphictyony cannot be later than 471/0, when Themistocles fled from Athens. Again, Diodorus[9] gives the death of Leotychidas and the accession of Archidamus as occurring in the archonship of Phaedon, 476/5. It would seem then that Diodorus has confused the dates of Leotychidas' exile and of his death, and has counted the years of his life in exile as part of his reign, as was done by him also in the case of Plistoanax.[10] Allowing for these corrections, the fleet would winter at Pagasae 477/6, the campaign taking place in the autumn of 477 or early spring of 476; the expulsion of the medizers was considered at the spring Pylaea of 476, and Leotychidas was tried in the summer of 476. Yet, after all, it is a strong temptation to follow Plutarch's account and place all these events in the year immediately following the battle of Plataea.

Though this Thessalian campaign failed in its attempt to punish the Aleuads, as well as in the probable further motive,

§ 1. 4. V² 259 n. 1; cf. Busolt III² 1 p. 83 n. 1.
§ 1. 5. Busolt II² 573 n. 5.
§ 1. 6. XI 48 2.
§ 1. 7. Thuc. III 1 1, 89 1; Diod. XI 48 2.
§ 1. 8. Plut. Them. 20; Busolt III² 1 p. 85 n. 2.
§ 1. 9. XI 48 2.
§ 1. 10. Diod. XIII 75 1.

namely the strengthening of Lacedaemonian influence in northern
Greece, it is clear that the Aleuadae preserved little more than the
shadow of their former might.　From this time on no Aleuad of
Larissa is heard of as tagus; and some twenty years later the
Pharsalian branch of the family is expelled from power.[11]　The
result must have been a great increase of power on the part of the
anti-Aleuad element and a great loss of prestige on the part of the
Aleuads.　The office of tagus, being an extraordinary one, was ap-
parently allowed to lapse and was revived only in the time of
Lycophron.

§ 2. When Cimon was besieging the Persians in Eïon, 476,
Menon, a wealthy Pharsalian, at the head of 300 of his penestae
whom he had armed at his own expense, joined him and aided
him in the prosecution of the siege.　He also contributed twelve
silver talents toward the expense of the campaign.　In return for
his services he was by decree of the Athenians presented with the
citizenship.[1]

§ 3. Not long after this, Cimon, in command of the Greek
fleet, stormed and took Scyrus, which was inhabited by Pelasgians
and Dolopes.　These people were rough and piratical, and caused
great trouble to the Thessalian merchants, not receiving trades-
men, but plundering all those who anchored near Ctesium.　At
last some merchants held in bonds escaped and going to the Am-
phictyons demanded that they exact the accustomed penalty of
Scyrus.　This was in the form of a money payment, but the mul-
titude refused to pay and bade those actually guilty of this particular act of piracy pay the sum.　To avoid this the latter sent
letters to Cimon, then at Eïon, offering to deliver the city to him
if he should come with the fleet.　This is the story of Plutarch;
but it seems more probable that Cimon's main motive in taking

§ 1. 11. Thuc. I 111 1.

§ 2. 1. Demos. XIII 23, XXIII 199.　While these passages might refer to
the operations against Brasidas in 424 (in which case Menon would be identical
with the leader of the Pharsalians who as allies came to Athens in 431; Thuc.
II 22 3), still at that time the influence of Daochus (cf. pp. 9 sq. infra) would
probably have prevented such assistance; and both the language and the context
of the passages cited from Demosthenes point to the earlier date.

the island was to seek the bones of Theseus, who according to the legend had there been treacherously done to death by Lycomedes. In 476, in the archonship of Phaedon, an oracle had directed the Athenians to bring to Athens the bones of Theseus and to pay him fitting honor as to a hero. The Dolopes refused to show Cimon where Theseus lay, or quite possibly denied any knowledge of his resting place. While seeking the tomb, the story goes, Cimon noticed an eagle screaming and tearing at a hillock; and on excavating there he found the remains of a huge body and beside it a spear and a sword of bronze. He brought them back to Athens in his own ship, and they were received there with great honors. The Scyrians were enslaved and the island became permanently an Athenian possession, with the land divided among cleruchs.[1]

The date of the seizure of Scyrus is in doubt. It may be placed in the year 475, immediately after the capture of Eïon by Cimon, as is done by Wilamowitz,[2] or in 474 to 472, as is done by Busolt.[3] The determination is not of vital consequence, as the event is not connected with other events.

§ 4. The weakening of the power of the Aleuads by the campaign of Leotychidas did not prevent the election of Echecratidas of Pharsalus as tagus.[1] He felt himself somewhat insecure in his position, for many remembered gratefully the weakening of the power of the Aleuad line by the Lacedaemonians, and when the relations between Athens and Sparta became strained, he did not let the opportunity slip to strengthen himself by an alliance with the former city. This alliance was brought about as follows:

The Messenians revolted from Sparta in 464, and fortified themselves on Mt. Ithome. After several years of fruitless siege the Lacedaemonians invited assistance from various cities, among them Athens, which sent a large force under Cimon. Soon, however, they began to fear that the Athenians might be persuaded over to the side of the Messenians, and dismissed them on the

§ 3. 1. Thuc. I 98 2; Diod. XI 60 2; Plut. Thes. 36, Cim. 8; Paus. I 17 6, III 3 7.

§ 3. 2. Aristoteles und Athen I 146.

§ 3. 3. III² 1 p. 105 n. 2, where arguments are given.

§ 4. 1. Thuc. I 111 1.

ground that their aid was not needed. The Athenians returned
home, but the insult rankled in their hearts and they formed an
alliance with the Argives, who were old rivals of the Lacedaemonians. The two cities then joined in an alliance on the same
terms with the Thessalians.[2] The hatred felt against Sparta by
the Aleuads of Larissa and of Pharsalus made them in their
capacity of leaders of the Thessalian state fall in zealously, while
the party opposed to them felt less readiness to join the enemies
of those who had attempted to destroy the tyrants.

§ 5. Shortly after this, the Lacedaemonians made an expedition
into Phocis to punish that nation for the invasion of the district
of Doris and for the taking of one of the Dorian cities. The
Athenians saw their opportunity to revenge themselves at the close
of the war by cutting off the return of the Lacedaemonian force.
With an army of 14000 men, in which were 1000 Argives and
a body of Thessalian horsemen, they occupied the passes over
Mt. Geranêa. The Lacedaemonians learned this, and did not
attempt to cross, but marched on to Tanagra and there encamped,
awaiting a favorable opportunity to pass through toward home.
The Athenians and their allies then advanced into Boeotia, and a
severe battle took place, in the midst of which the Thessalians
deserted to the enemy. The Athenians and the Argives fought
on bravely none the less, but though both sides suffered severe
losses the outcome was a decisive victory for the Lacedaemonians.[1]
This campaign took place in the late summer of 457.

Diodorus' account [2]— less trustworthy, of course — differs ma-
terially from that just given, which is the story of Thucydides.
According to him the battle was indecisive, and was closed only
by the coming of darkness. The two armies then encamped
opposite each other, and the Athenians arranged to draw provis-
ions from Attica. One night the Thessalians, intending to take
the Athenian camp by surprise in the darkness, fell by chance
upon a convoy of supplies. Those in charge of the supplies mis-
took the Thessalians for their friends, and so were at a great dis-

§ 4. 2. Thuc. 1 102 ; Paus. I 29 8 sq.
§ 5. 1. Thuc. I 107 sq. ; Herod. IX 35 ; Paus. I 29 9 ; Diod. XI 79 4–6.
§ 5. 2. XI 80.

advantage, being thrown into confusion while the enemy remained in perfect order. The Athenians in the camp however learned of the attack and came in haste, and drove off the Thessalians with heavy loss. Then the Lacedaemonians came to the aid of the Thessalians, and a long and bloody battle ensued, lasting all day, and closing only at the approach of night. The losses on both sides were heavy, but neither party had a decided advantage. Worn out by the conflict, the generals conferred, and concluded a truce of four months, which was virtually a victory for the Lacedaemonians, as it allowed them to reach home unhindered.

§ 6. A few years later, either 454 or 453,[1] an Athenian army under command of Myronides marched into Thessaly; on the way it was joined by the Boeotians and the Phocians,[2] then their allies. In undertaking this campaign the Athenians were moved by a desire for vengeance upon the Thessalians for their treachery at Tanagra, and also by the wish to restore to his native city Orestes, son of the tagus Echecratidas, their recent ally. The bearing of these events upon each other is probably that while the Thessalian detachment was serving in the Athenian army before the battle of Tanagra, Echecratidas died, and his son Orestes was refused the chief place in the city. Acnonius son of Aparus, an anti-Aleuad leader, now stood at the head of the state. Orestes was the leader of the faction allied with Athens; hence Acnonius was inimical to Athens and inclined toward Sparta. This change in the rule and in the political relations at home caused the desertion of the Thessalian troops to the Lacedaemonians at Tanagra. A short time later Acnonius felt himself strong enough to banish Orestes from his native city; the exile at once sought aid from his father's ally, Athens.

Acnonius son of Aparus appears, it is true, only in an inscription found at Delphi [3]; but there are strong grounds for believing him the leader of the party that expelled Orestes. He was tetrarch of the Thessalians, according to the inscription; and as he stood in the direct line four generations before the Daochus

§ 6. 1. Busolt III² 1 p. 333 and note.
§ 6. 2. Cf. CIA. IV p. 8 #22b.
§ 6. 3. Homolle in BCH. XXI (1897) 592–598.

who was Philip's ambassador to Thebes in 338,[4] and was grandfather of the Daochus who ruled all Thessaly from 431 to 404, as we shall see later, he must be placed at least as early as 455, while he cannot be placed earlier, since Echecratidas was then tagus.

Myronides easily penetrated as far as Pharsalus, but the city was closed to him, and he was obliged to invest it. By so doing he made no headway, for his army was master of only the ground in the immediate vicinity of the camp, and any detachments sent out were at once driven back by the Thessalian cavalry. Despairing of success, he soon raised the siege and returned to Athens with neither end of the invasion accomplished.[5] Orestes of necessity returned with him, and from that time on no member of his family held power at Pharsalus. In fact the Aleuads in all their branches now withdraw into the background. The Scopadae had almost perished in a great calamity about 500 B. C.; the Larissaean Aleuads were much weakened by the campaign of Leotychidas; the Pharsalian line was in exile. The Pelinnaean and Itonian branches never held much prominence. And while the Aleuadae of Larissa reappear as military commanders, as opponents of the Pheraean tyrants, and as minions of the Macedonian kings, they are never again heard of as "kings" or tagi of Thessaly.

§ 7. Some years after the expedition of Myronides, Pericles summoned a conference of all the Greeks to confer about the shrines destroyed by the Persians. Among those invited to attend it were the Thessalians, the Phthiot Achaeans, the Oetaeans and the Malians; but the opposition of the Lacedaemonians brought the project to naught.[1]

§ 8. A long period ensues of which we hear nothing. We may think of this time, lasting down to the opening of the Peloponnesian war, as one of comparative peace and quiet. The military tetrads developed into the tetrarchies, governments civil rather than military in their nature, at whose head stood tetrarchs.

§ 6. 4. Plut. Demos. 18.
§ 6. 5. Thuc. I 111 1; Diod. XI 83 3 sq.
§ 7. 1. Plut. Pericl. 17.

These were elected by a duly assembled congress of the district; the length of the term of office is not known. The only tetrarch of whom we hear by name in the times preceding the Peloponnesian war is the Acnonius already mentioned.

Three sons of Acnonius are known, Hagias, Telemachus and Agelaus. All these were famous athletes: Hagias won five victories at Nemea, three (or five) at Delphi, and five at the Isthmus; Telemachus won the same number of victories, and killed a Tyrrhenian in a wrestling match; Agelaus won the boys' stadium race at Delphi.[1]

§ 9. The Aleuadae gradually recovered some measure of their former power at Larissa, and while they were still rent by factions, they had a much firmer hold at the outbreak of the Peloponnesian war than they had had twenty-five to forty years earlier. Proof of this consists in the renewal of the old alliance of the Athenians and the Thessalians in 431. A force of cavalry was sent to help in the defense of Athens against the Lacedaemonians when the latter were about to invade Attica.[1] This force consisted of detachments from Larissa, Pharsalus, Pagasae,[2] Crannon, Pîresiae, Gyrton and Pherae, each under its own leader. Of the Larissaeans indeed there were two leaders, Polymedes and Aristonous, one from each faction of the Aleuadae, then nearly balanced in power in that city; and the Pharsalian leader was Menon,

§8. 1. Homolle in BCH. XXI (1897) 592–598, XXIII (1899) 421–485; Preuner ein delphischer Weihgeschenk.

§ 9. 1. Thuc. II 22 3.

§ 9. 2. Thuc. II 22 3. Codd. ACEFM here read Παράσιοι, B[G] Περάσιοι. The word may have crept in under the influence of the preceding Φαρσάλιοι and of the second word after it, Πειράσιοι. Accordingly some editors bracket the word, others read Παράλιοι (a people of Malis, who are clearly not the ones meant — Thuc. III 92 2), and Stahl reads Παγασαῖοι. The second word after it is Πειράσιοι. Πειρασία in Magnesia, mentioned by Steph. Byz. s. v., would give this form of the adjective, but the place is unimportant and no town of that rocky peninsula would have cavalry to send. Most editors read Πυράσιοι; but Apoll. Rhod. I 37 mentions a place Πειρεσιαί (the Homeric Ἀστέριον) in central Thessaly, which occurs also in several other authors (Steph. Byz. s. v. Asterium; Hom. Il. II 735; Strabo 438 sq.; Orph. Arg. 164; Liv. XXXII 13 9 Iresiae). This place would more probably send a detachment than would Pyrasus, the seaport of Phthiotid Thebes, which itself did not take part in the campaign.

who, as his name does not occur in the Daochid line (thus we shall term the family of Acnonius, from its most prominent members), seems to belong to a family of an opposing faction. This indicates that the Daochid line — hostile to the Athenians on account of their alliance with the Echecratids — was for the time displaced by the family of which Menon was a member, which had gradually grown into prominence since the expulsion of Orestes. We should therefore expect Menon to be friendly to the Athenians, and such we actually find him.

Soon after the entrance of the Lacedaemonians into Attica there occurred near Phrygii a severe skirmish between a company of Athenian horsemen and the Thessalians on the one side and the Boeotian cavalry on the other. The latter had the worse of it until some hoplites came to their aid, when they turned the Athenians and Thessalians to flight and inflicted some loss upon them. The vanquished succeeded however in recovering the dead on the same day without the necessity of resorting to a truce, and the Peloponnesians erected a trophy on the next day. The tomb of the Thessalians who fell in this battle was still to be seen in the time of Pausanias beside the road leading to the Academy.[3]

§ 10. With this one incident closes the participation of the Thessalians in the main current of the Peloponnesian war. Remarkable as this is, it is to be explained by an inscription found at Delphi :[1]

"I am Daochus, son of Hagias; my fatherland is Pharsalus; I was archon of all Thessaly, not through force but by law, for twenty-seven years ; and Thessaly teemed with a bounteous and fruitful peace and wealth."

Daochus, legal ruler of all Thessaly, was grandfather of the Daochus who was Philip's partisan in Thessaly 355 to 338.[2] His archonship must therefore fall in about the period of the Peloponnesian war. Further, his twenty-seven years of power cannot have ended later than 404, when Lycophron attempted to render

§ 9. 3. Thuc. II 22 2 sq. ; Paus. I 29 6.
§ 10. 1. Homolle in BCH. XXI (1897) 592–598.
§ 10. 2. Plut. Demos. 18 ; Demos. XVIII 295 ; Polyb. XVII 14 4 ; Harpoc. s. v. Daochus ; CIGIns. III 251.

himself tyrant of Thessaly,[3] for Daochus' rule was one of peace
and prosperity, so the epigram tells us; and as no mention of
Daochus occurs in the account of the campaign of 431, we are
forced to believe that he was then not yet archon. Between 431
and 404 is a period of just twenty-seven years; and we may
fairly suppose that in a council of the Thessalian league, held in
the year 431, Daochus was elected archon, and that to him, as he
represented the anti-Athenian party, is due the change in the
attitude of Thessaly during the war. We must acknowledge that
his influence was not exerted in favor of Sparta; but at the same
time the division in the feelings of the Thessalians and a probable
desire on his own part to promote the material prosperity of his
country afford a reasonable explanation of his neutral position.
In the matter of Brasidas' and Rhamphias' marches[4] through
Thessaly, the opposition offered to the Lacedaemonians was doubtless due to the recent founding of Heraclêa, upon the borders of
Thessaly, which was regarded as an aggression on the part of the
Lacedaemonians. That however there resided at Pharsalus in 424
a power upon which Brasidas relied for permission to cross the
country, is shown by the fact that he sent ahead a messenger to
that city to ask free passage for himself and his army.[5] This
power must have been Daochus.

§ 11. In the early months of 428 the Thracian Sitalces took the
field against the Macedonian Perdiccas, and advanced into Macedonia and Chalcidice. Perdiccas was able to offer no effective resistance, and the northern Greeks began to fear that he might proceed also into their territories. Accordingly the Thessalians, the
Phthiot Achæans, the Magnetes and the other tribes dependent
upon the Thessalians, including those who dwelt in the Sperchîus
valley, mustered and remained under arms for some weeks, until
as the Athenians failed to send him their promised support Sitalces felt constrained to make peace with Perdiccas. Upon the dis-
persal of his army homeward, the Thessalians also resumed the
pursuits of peace, as there no longer existed occasion for fear.[1]

§ 10. 3. Xen. Hell. II 3 4.
§ 10. 4. Thuc. IV 78, V 13.
§ 10. 5. Thuc. IV 78 1.
§ 11. 1. Thuc. II 101; Diod. XII 51.

§ 12. In the early part of the summer of 426 there was a series of earthquakes, which did immense damage in the neighborhood of the Malian gulf. Most of the buildings of Lamia, Phalara, Echinus and Larissa Cremaste, of Trachis, and of the coast towns of Locris and Boeotia were thrown down, and much loss of life occurred. A great wave swept the coasts, reaching as far as Peparethus, by which time it had spent its force; the city of that name however had its city wall, the Prytanêum and some other buildings shaken down. The Sperchîus was turned from its channel into the roads and fields, and the Boagrius was changed into another ravine; and the hot springs of Thermopylae and those at Aedepsus in Euboea ceased to flow for three days. [1]

There had been for years a state of war between the Trachinians and the Oetaeans, and the former had lost the greater part of their citizens; with the new disaster of the earthquake they were entirely helpless. For aid they looked first toward Athens, but they feared that that city might not be faithful to them in time of need. Therefore they joined with the people of Doris, who also were much wasted by war with the Oetaeans, in an embassy to the Lacedaemonians. Tisamenus was the spokesman of the Trachinians; and on hearing his plea the Lacedaemonians were much inclined to grant the request for help, both on the sentimental grounds that Doris was the mother-city of all Dorians and that Heracles their ancestor had settled at Trachis, and on the practical ground that a strong colony there would serve as a base for a naval force to act against Euboea, and as a station on the way to Thrace. The god at Delphi was consulted and proved favorable; and at his bidding they sent as colonists both Lacedaemonians and perioeci, and invited all other Greeks except the Ionians, Achaeans and a few others to join them. Such was the confidence in the Lacedaemonians that volunteers assembled in great numbers; and the colonists, led by the Lacedaemonians Leon, Alcidas and Damagon, amounted in all to 10000, of whom 4000 were from Laconia and the rest of the Peloponnesus, and 6000 from other regions. The new city was founded twenty stades from the shore, six stades

§ 12. 1. Thuc. III 89; Strabo 60.

from the former Trachis and forty stades from Thermopylae, and was named Ἡράκλεια Τραχινία or ἐν Τραχῖνι.[2] The building of dockyards was begun, and the pass at Thermopylae was fortified and kept under guard. The Athenian fear of a descent upon Euboea was not however realized, for the various Thessalian nations, dreading so powerful a neighbor and regarding it as a trespasser upon their land, gathered in force and made a constant war upon the new city, which greatly weakened it. The mismanagement of the Lacedaemonian officials also had a bad effect upon the city, and many colonists deserted; so that in its relations to its neighbors it was kept on the defensive. It was nevertheless still strong enough in the autumn to contribute 500 of the 3000 hoplites sent by the allies of the Lacedaemonians, under Lacedaemonian commanders, to aid the Aetolians in their resistance to the invasion of the Athenian Demosthenes and the Acarnanians.[3]

§ 13. In the summer of 424 Brasidas was sent out with 1700 hoplites from Sparta to Chalcidice. His march to Heraclêa Trachinia was through friendly country; but thence onward he had to cross Thessaly, which while taking no part in the war had a faction friendly to the Athenians, as we have seen; and though the archon Daochus was friendly to Sparta, the motives of such a large force in crossing the country would arouse suspicion, the more so from the recent establishment of Heraclêa on the borders of the country. Brasidas, realizing this, halted at Heraclêa and sent ahead a messenger to Pharsalus to ask free passage for himself and his army. To give reply there came to Melitêa in Phthiotis Panaerus, Dorus, Hippolochidas, Tarylaus and Strophacus, a proxenus of the Chalcidians. Brasidas advanced under the guidance of certain Thessalians, among them Niconidas of Larissa, a friend of the Macedonian Perdiccas (whom Brasidas wished to join). On reaching Melitêa he was informed that the Thessalians had decided to refuse him passage; but none the less he kept on, disregarding the natural difficulties of the country, and reached the Enipeus river without resistance. Here however a

§ 12. 2. For the history of this city see R. Weil, die Oetaea, in Hermes VII (1873) 380–392.
§ 12. 3. Thuc. III 92 sq., 100, V 51; Diod. XII 59 3–5; Strabo 428 sq.

force of Thessalians blocked his march, and the guides declared their disinclination and inability to lead him farther against the will of the natives. Brasidas now explained to his opponents that he came as a friend to the Thessalians, and as an enemy not to them, but to the Athenians only ; that the Thessalians and the Lacedaemonians were at peace and he saw no reason why they should not use each other's land peacefully ; and that he would not proceed against their will, for he was unable to do so, but he did not think it right for them to check him. On hearing this the Thessalians dispersed ; and Brasidas, at the bidding of the guides, advanced rapidly and that night encamped beside the Apidanus ; on the following day he reached Phacium, and on the next entered Perrhaebia, before any further resistance could be concerted. The Perrhaebians gave him guidance to Dium, the border city of the kingdom of Perdiccas, at the foot of Olympus.[1]

§ 14. In the winter after this, 424/3, the Boeotians obtained javelin-throwers and slingers from the region of the Malian gulf to aid them and their allies against the Athenians at Delium. These troops were present in the conflict resulting in the Athenian defeat and withdrawal.[1]

§ 15. At the time of the battle of Amphipolis (422), in which Brasidas fell, reinforcements consisting of 900 hoplites commanded by the Spartans Rhamphias, Autocharidas and Epicydidas were on their way to him. At Heraclêa they delayed to try to straighten out the affairs of that troubled city, and at this time occurred the battle of Amphipolis. As winter came on, Rhamphias proceeded into Thessaly as far as Cierium [1] ; but he met with stout resistance, and as news came that Brasidas was dead and that the Athenians had withdrawn from Chalcidice, there was no longer need of his force, both sides being weary of war and inclined toward peace,

§ 13. 1. Thuc. IV 78, 79 1.
§ 14. 1. Thuc. IV 100 1.
§ 15. 1. The name is given in Thuc. V 13 1 as Pierium ; but coins with the legend ΚΙΕΡΙΕΙΩΝ have been found in this district, which makes it clear that in the local dialect the name is properly Cierium. Muret in BCH.V (1881) 288.

and he returned home without essaying a farther northward march.[2]

§ 16. The enmity between the Heracleots and their neighbors, seemingly for a time quiescent, now broke out afresh, in the early winter of 420/19. The Aenianes, Dolopes, Malians and some other Thessalians assailed the city and in battle defeated the defenders with considerable loss, including that of the Lacedaemonian leader, Xenagoras the Cnidian. Besieged within the city, the survivors sent to the Boeotians for aid. The Thebans, fearing that the Athenians might seize the place while the Lacedaemonians were busy in the Peloponnesus, willingly responded with 1000 hoplites. With the assistance of these the besiegers were driven off. The Thebans then took charge of the city and expelled the Lacedaemonian governor Hegesippidas for mismanagement. By this course, though it was taken in the interests of the city, the Thebans incurred the anger of the Lacedaemonians, and as when we next hear of Heraclêa it is in Lacedaemonian control, it is to be presumed that it was given up to them by the Boeotians after more or less of argument and possibly of conflict.[1]

Some years later (413/2) the Lacedaemonian king Agis made a winter campaign from Decelêa into Thessaly. He first ravaged the country of the Oetaeans, recovering much of the booty that they had in their recent conflicts taken from the Heracleots, and exacting in addition a heavy indemnity from them. For the farther protection of Heraclêa he compelled the Phthiot Achaeans and other southern Thessalians to give hostages and to pay tribute in money; and while the remaining Thessalians blamed their conduct they were unable to resist. The hostages were sent to Corinth and influence was brought upon them to enter the Lacedaemonian alliance[2]; and the Achaeans seem to have yielded, for three years later they were found upon the side of the Heracleots against the Achaeans. However an unwilling ally is worse than no ally at all, as the Heracleots learned to their cost. Relying upon them, they made ready to war upon the Oetaeans;

§ 15. 2. Thuc. V 12 sq., 14 1.
§ 16. 1. Thuc. V 51, 52 1; Diod. XII 77 4.
§ 16. 2. Thuc. VIII 3 1.

but when they were all arrayed for battle, the Achaeans betrayed them and 700 Heracleots fell, including Labotas the harmost from Lacedaemon.[3]

§ 17. Here closes this period in the history of Thessaly; for the next event of which we hear concerns Lycophron of Pherae, and with it the eventful epoch of the tyrants of Pherae is begun. But we may mention certain other events occurring in Thessaly during the Peloponnesian war, known only from casual references. Amynias was sent as ambassador to that country shortly before 422[1]; possibly to oppose Brasidas' passage. Andocides also went on an embassy to that country, and was accused of making trouble there.[2] During the time of the Peloponnesian war must have taken place the hospitable entertainment of the sophist Gorgias of Leontini by the Aleuad Aristippus, who, as well as the other Thessalians, was much taken with the new learning.[3] In 406 Critias, the Athenian tyrant, known favorably in Thessaly as a teacher of sophistic learning, tried to stir up the penestae against their masters, being assisted in this by one Prometheus.[4] Eurylochus, an Aleuad of Larissa, and Scopas of Crannon both unsuccessfully invited Socrates to make his home with them.[5] Scopas also sent a valuable necklace as a present to Cyrus the Younger.[6]

§16. 3. Xen. Hell. I 2 18. These Achaeans are generally supposed to have been the Achaeans who were excluded from participation in the founding of the city; and it is assumed that they were later admitted to the rights of citizenship. This assumption is purely gratuitous, and in any case the defection of a slight incoming element could hardly have produced such a serious effect upon the fortunes of the battle. Cf. Thirlwall Hist. Greece IV 95 and note.

§ 17. 1. Aristoph. Vespae 1270–1274; Eupolis fr. 209 Kock ap. Schol. Aristoph. Vesp. 1271; Harwardt de irrision. II 12; Starkie ad Aristoph. Vesp. 74.

§ 17. 2. Andoc. IV 41; Lysias VI 6.

§ 17. 3. Isoc. XV 155; Plato Meno 70 AB; Cic. Orat. 176; Philost. Vit. Soph. i (Gorg.) p. 203, xvi (Crit.) p. 213, Ep. p. 364.

§ 17. 4. Philost. Vit. Soph. xvi (Crit.) p. 213; Xen. Hell. II 3 36.

§ 17. 5. Diog. Laert. II 25.

§ 17. 6. Aelian. Var. Hist. XII 1.

APPENDIX I.

THE RULING FAMILIES OF PHARSALUS.

§ 1. Of Pharsalus we learn that it was ruled by an oligarchy, which however governed the dependent territories and cities wisely and thus maintained their city's leadership unassailed.[1] The city also had an excellent law requiring any citizen to assist the officials with his counsel if called upon.[2] Just who the oligarchs were has however been rather obscure. We shall endeavor to show that there were three lines, the Echecratid, the Daochid and the Menonid families.

§ 2. The earliest Echecratidas is the Larissaean who dedicated at Delphi a small Apollo, which was reputed to be earlier than any of the other votive offerings[1] — hence earlier than those of Solon and of Croesus. It was probably his grandson of the same name who was the husband of Dyseris and father of the wealthy Antiochus.[2] Echecratia, wife of Creon and mother of the second Scopas,[3] was, if we may judge from chronology and name, a sister of the second Echecratidas. Antiochus ruled for thirty years in Pharsalus, part of which time he was tagus of Thessaly. He hospitably entertained the poets Simonidas and Anacreon. As he thus represented the main power in the country, he was visited by the celebrated Ionian hetaera Thargelia, who endeavored to make him friendly toward the Persians.[4] He died however before their coming, and the office of tagus was transferred to the Larissaean Thorax. After the campaign of Leotychidas, the Pharsalian Echecratidas (third of the name) son of Antiochus was

§ 1. 1. Aristot. Pol. V 5 7 p. 1306a ; Xen. Hell. VI 1 8.
§ 1. 2. Plato Sisyphus 387 B.
§ 2. 1. Paus. X 16 8.
§ 2. 2. Simonides 48 Schneidewin apud Ael. Arist. p. 127 D ; Anacreon 103, 109 Bergk ; Schol. Theoc. XVI 34.
§ 2. 3. Schol. Theoc. XVI 36.
§ 2. 4. Theoc. XVI 34 et Sch. ; Simonides 48 Schneidewin apud Ael. Arist. p. 127 D; Phot. s. v. Thargelia ; Plut. Pericl. 24 ; Philost. Ep. p. 364.

chosen tagus, but his son Orestes was banished from home about 454. The Athenians unsuccessfully attempted to restore him.[5]

This is the story of the Aleuads of Pharsalus, as it is generally accepted; but there are in it some difficulties which many historians fail to notice. If we reckon back from the known date of Orestes and from the approximate date given by the relations of Antiochus with Anacreon and Simonides, the second Echecratidas would come about 560–540, and the first one about 620. Yet Echecratidas I. is a Larissaean, and the only connection of the family with Pharsalus is that implied by the campaign of Myronides against Pharsalus. The statement of Quintilian[6] that he was uncertain whether the scene of the calamity of the Scopadae was Crannon or Pharsalus is entirely irrelevant. In fact, the manner in which Theocritus[7] groups Antiochus and Aleuas together, and speaks of the Scopadae of Crannon separately, would of itself give the impression that Antiochus was a native of Larissa. Thus all depends upon the Thucydidean account of Orestes, without which no one would ever have thought of connecting the Echecratids with Pharsalus. It is certain that there were rival factions at Larissa as early as the middle of the sixth century, for Simus, father of Aleuas and grandfather of Thorax, hired foreign guards on account of such troubles.[8] Does it not seem likely then that the expulsion of Orestes was a culmination of such dissensions? But why then did Myronides not direct his army upon Larissa, if Orestes was exiled from that city and not from Pharsalus? The military science of his day would have permitted him to leave

§ 2. 5. Thuc. I 111 1.

§ 2. 6. XI 2 14; cf. Chapter III § 7 n.1 above. [Viz.: § 7. 1. Callim. Epig. 64 3–6; Cic. de Orat. II 352 sq.; Val. Max. I 8 ext. 7; Quint. XI 2 11–16; Phaed. Fab. IV 25; Ovid. Ibis 511 sq. Quint. XI 2 14 says that Apollodorus, Eratosthenes, Euphorion and Eurypylus of Larissa all placed the disaster at Pharsalus; that Apollas and Callimachus placed it at Crannon; and that the latter version gained currency merely through the fact that Cicero adopted it in preference to the former. However Herod. VI 127 and Theoc. XVI 36–39 place the seat of power of the Scopadae at Crannon, and while there is a possibility that the Scopadae ruled also at Pharsalus, the view is generally adopted that the Scopadae ruled at Crannon alone and that the Echecratids were in power at Pharsalus. Cf. Appendix I.]

§ 2. 7. XVI 34–39.

§ 2. 8. Aristot. Pol. V 5 9 p. 1306a.

Pharsalus untaken in his rear and to advance upon Larissa. It seems therefore that we must accept Orestes and his father as Pharsalians; and as Theocritus in the passage mentioned does not compel us to place Antiochus in the same city as Aleuas, we may carry the establishment of the line in that city back to the second Echecratidas. Probably this one, who would be contemporary with Simus, was expelled by the latter from Larissa when the factional troubles became sharp; but by previous friendly relations with Pharsalus he was able to take up his abode there, and to become the leader in the city. Removal from sight probably worked an improvement in the relations of the Aleuad lines, for both Echecratids and Larissaean Aleuads were on friendly terms with Athens; but the factions in Larissa evidently continued to exist,[9] or a new split in the family occurred at a later date.

The genealogical tree of this family has already been given as that of one branch of the Aleudae.[10]

§ 3. The second family[1] is that which began with Acnonius son of Aparus. He was tetrarch of Thessaliotis, and had three sons, Hagias, Telemachus and Agelaus, all famous athletes. Hagias' son was Daochus (I.), whose election as archon of Thessaly

§ 2. 9. Thuc. II 22 3.

§ 2. 10. Cap. II § 4. Here repeated:

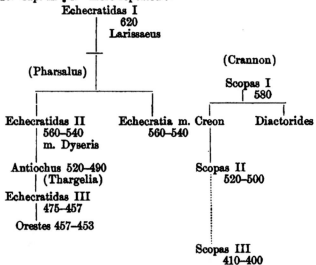

§ 3. 1. Homolle in BCH. XXI (1897) 592–598, XXIII (1899) 421–485; Preuner ein delphischer Weihgeschenk; Michel Recueil 1281.

brought the Thessalians to a neutral position in the Peloponnesian war. It was to him that Brasidas sent envoys asking free passage through Thessaly.[2] At his death Lycophron of Pherae rose into prominence.[3] Daochus' son Sisyphus (I.) "never fled the foe nor received a wound"; possibly it was he who gave the name to the spurious Platonic dialogue. We hear of one Athenaeus of Eretria who was his servant and flatterer.[4] Agelaus, probably grandson of the athlete, was archon of the Thessalian federation in 361/0 and contracted an alliance with the Athenians against Alexander of Pherae.[5] Daochus (II.), son of Sisyphus I., was the tool and minion of Philip of Macedonia, and aided in bringing Thessaly under his power. By his favor Daochus became tetrarch; and he was one of Philip's ambassadors to Thebes in 338. He was also a proxenus of the Anaphaeans.[6] He erected at Pharsalus a group of eight figures, representing himself and members of his family, in commemoration of their exploits. The figures were of bronze and were the work of Lysippus. A marble replica of the group was set up at Delphi, where it was found by the French excavators, along with eight inscriptions, which give us the greater part of our information about this family. Sisyphus (II.) was the son of Daochus II.

The Daochid line is therefore composed of the following members :

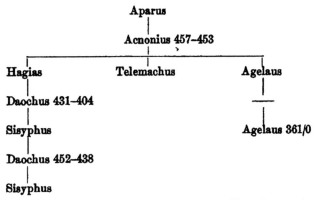

§ 3. 2. Thuc. IV 78 1.   § 3. Xen. Hell. II 3 4.

§ 3. 4. Theop. 20 apud Athen. 252 F.

§ 3. 5. Köhler in Ath. Mitt. II (1877) 197–213, 291.

§ 3. 6. Plut. Demos. 18; Harpoc. s. v.; Polyb. XVII 14 4: Demos. XVIII 295; CIG Ins. III 251.

§ 4. That fractional dissensions existed in Pharsalus long after the expulsion of the Echecratids is shown by the seizure of the place by Medius and the subsequent massacre of the mercenaries whom he left there, as well as by the express statement of Xenophon.[1]   From this we are enabled to posit another powerful family in the city.   We find this in the line of Menons and Thucydidae.

In 431 the Pharsalian detachment in the Thessalian force sent to the assistance of Athens was led by a Menon.[2]   Another Menon of Pharsalus led the Thessalians in the Lamian war (323–321), and fell in the final conflict; his daughter Phthia became the wife of the Epirot king Aeacides and the mother of Pyrrhus.[3] Marcellinus,[4] quoting from the De Arce of Polemon, mentions a Thucydides of Pharsalus, whose father's name was Menon.   The Menon here mentioned would probably be the most famous of that name in that city, namely the one who fell in the Lamian war.   From this another Thucydides of Pharsalus may be brought into the family, who was an Athenian proxenus and helped quell a riot at Athens in the year 411.[5]   He would be the son of the Menon first mentioned.   From Demosthenes[6] we learn that a Menon of Pharsalus took the field with 300 of his penestae, whom he himself equipped, and with these aided the Athenians under Cimon in the operations against Eïon.   This may be the grand-father of the Menon of the year 431.   Still another is the Menon who led the Thessalian troops of Cyrus.   Diodorus[7] says that he was a Larissaean, but from Xenophon[8] it is evident that he was a free lance, and he probably was merely a commander of mercenaries who had drifted to Larissa and there remained so long that he came to be spoken of as a native of the place.   His age would

§ 4. 1. Diod. XIV 82 5 sq.; Aristot. Anim. Hist. IX 31; Xen. Hell. VI 1 2.

§ 4. 2. Thuc. II 22 3.

§ 4. 3. Diod. XVIII 15 4, 17 6, 38 5 sq.; Plut. Pyrrh. 1, Phoc. 25.

§ 4. 4. Vita Thuc. 28.

§ 4. 5. Thuc. VIII 92 8.

§ 4. 6. Demos. XIII 23, XXIII 199.

§ 4. 7. XIV 19 8.

§ 4. 8. Anab. I sq. passim; v. et Appendix IV.

indicate that he was, if of the Pharsalian family, a brother of the Athenian proxenus Thucydides.

The Menonid line is thus composed:

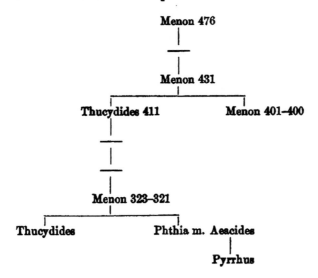

APPENDIX II.

THE RELATIONS BETWEEN THESSALY AND ATHENS.

§ 1. It has been generally supposed that the Athenians and the common people of Thessaly were in sympathy with each other, while the aristocratic families were on good terms with Sparta. This mistaken idea has led even Busolt into certain evident inconsistencies. In speaking of the treaty of Athens and Argos with the Thessalians in 462, he says: " Darauf schlossen diese beiden Staaten noch gemeinsam ein auf denselben Bedingungen beruhendes Bündnis mit den Thessalern ab, unter denen namentlich die mächtigen Aleuaden, wegen des Feldzuges des Leotychidas den Lakedaimoniern grollten."[1] This statement, which is perfectly justified, he at once proceeds to contradict in a footnote on the same page: " Auch mit dem Fürstenhause von Pharsalos unterhielten die Athener nähere Beziehungen. Thuk. I, 111. Der ritterschaftliche Adel war lakonisch gesinnt, während die demokratische Volksmenge mit den Athenern sympathisierte (Thuk. I, 107, 7; IV, 78, 3; Xen. Hell. II, 3, 36)." Yet if the " Fürstenhaus von Pharsalos " and the Aleuadae were not part and parcel of " der ritterschaftliche Adel," it would be hard to find aristocrats anywhere; and it is exceedingly questionable if any truly democratic party existed in Thessaly at that time. We may note in passing that of the three passages cited at the end of the extract only the second really bears upon the point: it will be discussed later. A few pages farther on, Busolt[2] says: " Der lakonerfreundliche Adel hatte dort die Oberhand gewonnen und auch den pharsalischen Fürsten Orestes, Sohn des Thessaler-Königs Echecratidas, vertrieben." This sentence either contains within itself the same inconsistency or is in contradiction with his previous statements.

§1. 1. Busolt III[2] 1 pp. 297 sq.
§ 1. 2. III[2] 1 p. 332.

§ 2. Let us now consider what alliances and enmities there were between the Athenians and the Pharsalians. Passing over the legendary friendship of Theseus and Pirithous, we come to the alliance of the Pisistratids with the Aleuadae, and to the aid received by Hippias from Cineas and his cavalry.[1] Here was an alliance of tyrant and aristocratic family — and it was exercised against Sparta. After the Persian wars it was the Lacedaemonians who tried to punish the Aleuads for medizing, while the Athenians, whose enmity to Sparta was growing, had some thoughts of cutting off the return of the Lacedaemonians from Thessaly.[2] Thus while Sparta won the gratitude of those not in power, she earned the hatred of the ruling element, and but a short time later Menon of Pharsalus, clearly a wealthy aristocrat, aided the Athenians at Eïon.[3] When the breach between Athens and Sparta widened, Athens secured the alliance of the Aleuads of Larissa and Pharsalus, who still remembered the campaign of Leotychidas. The appearance of a new element, viz. of the Daochid Acnonius, brought about a change in affairs. Acnonius was the opponent of the Echecratid line, hence hostile to Athens. To his charge may be laid the treachery of the Thessalian cavalry at Tanagra and the expulsion of the Aleuad Orestes, whom Athens vainly tried to restore.[4]

§ 3. When in 431 the Thessalian cities sent aid to Athens,[1] Polymedes and Aristonous, Aleuads of Larissa, led the troops of their own city, and Menon led the Pharsalians ; Pagasae, Crannon, Gyrton and Pherae all were cities of Pelasgiotis, dominated by Larissa, and Piresiae, the only other city taking part in the campaign, lay on the borderland between the territories of Larissa and of Pharsalus, and evidently followed the lead of one or of the other. Again it is the Aleuads who are friendly to Athens ; the Menonids of Pharsalus we have already seen to be on good terms with that city. But the election of Daochus as archon[2]

§ 2. 1. V. Cap. III § 4, § 6.
§ 2. 2. V. p. 2 supra.
§ 2. 3. V. p. 3 supra.
§ 2. 4. V. pp. 6 sq. supra.
§ 3. 1. Thuc. II 22.
§ 3. 2. V. pp. 9 sq. supra.

put an end to any alliance between Athens and Thessaly. Daochus was the grandson of Acnonius, whom Athens had fought
some twenty years before, and was hostile to that city. Yet the
presence of two factions in Thessaly prevented him from taking
active part in the war; he sought rather to preserve the prosperity of his country and keep the war, raging among the other
Greeks, from entering within the limits of his country. But when
the Lacedaemonians founded Heraclêa Trachinia, it was a patent
trespass upon the lands of the Thessalian league, and a local war
ensued, partly from this cause and partly as a continuation of the
old war between the Trachinians and the Oetaeans[3]; it is entirely
apart from the current of the Peloponnesian war.

On account of these local troubles Brasidas considered it doubt-
ful whether he would be allowed to cross the country; but he
sent a messenger on to Pharsalus to ask permission. After the
matter of Heraclêa sentiment was strong against permitting any
passage of armed forces through the land, and the request was
refused. When Brasidas advanced he was met by force; yet
when he declared that he came as a friend to the Thessalians,
and as an enemy only to Athens, and that the Thessalians and
the Lacedaemonians were at peace and there was no reason why
they should not use each other's lands for peaceful purposes, the
resistance dispersed and he marched on to Macedonia.[4] From
this it is clear that there was no alliance of any kind between
the Athenians and the Thessalians at that time; for had there
been, Brasidas' open avowal of hostility to the Athenians would
have been equivalent to a declaration of war upon the Thessalians,
as treaties in those days regularly included an express mention of
the allies of both parties, making an attack upon any one an
aggression against all. Niconidas of Larissa, Brasidas' guide, was
probably an Aleuad; why he, being of a family friendly to Athens,
should act in that capacity is not clear. He was however a friend
to Perdiccas, to whom Brasidas wished to go; and it is noticeable
that he did not enter very heartily into his task, for as soon as

§ 3. 3. V. pp. 11 sq., 14 supra.
§ 3. 4. Thuc. IV 78; v. pp. 12 sq. supra.

the way was blocked he declared that he could not and would not lead him farther. The opposition to Rhamphias some years later [5] may be traced to the uneasiness produced by the founding of Heraclêa and to the desire to keep aloof from the war.

§ 4. Certain other events throw little if any light on the relations of Athens and Thessaly at this time. The Thessalians were terrified at the advance of the Athenian ally Sitalces of Thrace and rose in arms to resist him [1]; but even if they had been in alliance with the Athenians they could not have relied upon the latter to retrain such a totally irresponsible party as the Thracian king. Both Andocides and Amynias were sent on embassies to Thessaly,[2] but the purpose of their missions is unknown. The tyrant Critias tried to cause an uprising among the penestae,[3] but he was anything rather than a democrat, and his doings cannot be taken to indicate any relations between the democracies of the two countries. On this point F. Pahle [4] says : "grund hierzu für Kritias war wol der, dasz der thessalische adel mit der athenischen demokratie verbündet war und er also als oligarch dessen macht gebrochen zu sehen wünschte. solcher landesverrath war ja am schlusz des peloponnesischen krieges von seiten der athenischen oligarchie ganz an der tagesordnung." Herein, while he refers to an alliance which did not at that time exist, he takes the correct view of Thessalo-Athenian relations in general. A campaign of Astyphilus into Thessaly at some time shortly after the Corinthian war [5] gives no light, as it is unkown in whose favor it was undertaken.

§ 5. Political conditions changed rapidly between 404 and 375. The next relations of Athens with Thessaly are the alliances with the tyrant Jason in 373,[1] and again with the tyrant

§ 3. 5. V. p. 13 supra.
§ 4. 1. V. p. 10 supra.
§ 4. 2. V. p. 15 supra.
§ 4. 3. Xen. Hell. II 3 36.
§ 4. 4. In Fleckeisen's Jrb. f. klass. Phil. XII (1866) 531 n. 2.
§ 4. 5. Isaeus IX 14.
§ 5. 1. V. Cap. VI §§ 11 sq. [References: Xen. Hell. VI 1 10–12; Schäfer Demos. u. s. Zeit I² 58, 62; Köhler in Hermes V (1871) 8–10; CIA. II 88; Demos. XLIX 10, 22, 24, 31, 62; Nepos Timoth. 4 2 sq.]

Alexander in 368,[2] the latter directed notably against the other
Thessalians and their allies the Thebans.   Here is a clear case of
alliance with the oligarchic party, nay even with the house of
tyrants.   However, the aggressions of Alexander upon Peparethus
caused the Athenians to unite with the Thessalian league, at whose
head then stood the Daochid Agelaus.[3]   But soon they parted;
and opposition to the Pheraeans united the Daochids and the
Aleuads, who bowed to Philip, aided him in the expulsion of the
last of the tyrants of Pherae, and brought Thessaly into his
power.   In the Second Sacred War Athens, Sparta and Phocis
fought the Thessalians, the Boeotians and Philip.   In 338 the
Thessalians were eager to take the field against Athens[4]; and a
great battle took place at Chaeronêa, where Philip's forces routed
the Athenians and their allies.   Later the Thessalians under
command of Menon joined the Athenians and others in the
Lamian war, 323–321.

In all this we see that the Aleuad family, in its various branches,
and the Menonids of Pharsalus were consistently on good terms
with Athens.   On the other hand the Daochids of Pharsalus were
opposed to that city.   This is true to the greatest degree down
to the end of the fifth century, while in the fourth the events of
the time had more effect upon their relations.

§ 6. There remains to be considered the one passage that lends
color to the belief that it was the democratic or popular element
in Thessaly that allied itself with the Athenians.   Thucydides
IV 78 2 sq. says, in reference to Brasidas' desire to traverse
Thessaly, "καὶ τοῖς πᾶσί γε ὁμοίως Ἕλλησιν ὕποπτον καθειστήκει
τὴν τῶν πέλας μὴ πείσαντας διιέναι· τοῖς τε Ἀθηναίοις αἰεί ποτε τὸ
πλῆθος τῶν Θεσσαλῶν εὔνουν ὑπῆρχεν. ὥστε εἰ μὴ δυναστείᾳ μᾶλ-
λον ἢ ἰσονομίᾳ ἐχρῶντο τὸ ἐγχώριον οἱ Θεσσαλοί, οὐκ ἂν ποτε
προῆλθεν." "The traversing of one's neighbors' lands without per-

§ 5. 2. V. Cap. VI § 24. [References: Demos. XXIII 120; Diod. XV
71 3; Harpoc. s. v. Alexander; Ephippus fr. 1 Kock ap. Athen. 112 F;
Köhler in Ath. Mitt. II (1877) 291; Plut. Pelop. 31, Mor. 193 DE.]
§ 5. 3. V. Cap. VI §§ 29–31. [References: Demos. L 4, LI 8; Xen.
Hell. V 4 35; Diod. XV 95 1–3; Köhler in Ath. Mitt. II (1877) 197–213,
291; Polyaen. VI 2 1–2.]
§ 5. 4. Aesch. III 161.

mission was a well established cause of suspicion among all the Greeks alike. The majority of the Thessalians was ever friendly to the Athenians; so that he would not have proceeded had not the Thessalians been under an illegally usurped government rather than under a form of rule constituted legally and in accordance with their local custom." 'Ισονομία and δυναστεία are here merely the legal and illegal forms of ὀλιγαρχία, [1] the normal government of the country, and the πλῆθος must be the majority of those who were of consequence and possessed the franchise, not of the penestae and of others who had no voice in the government. Thus it was a question of oligarchic factions and not of strife between the aristocracy and democracy, for there is no reason to suppose that there existed a true democracy in Thessaly at that time. The passage therefore means that Brasidas in advancing relied upon the favor of Daochus, the enemy of Athens, and that Thucydides regarded Daochus as having gained his position by irregular methods. Yet the inscription at Delphi [2] speaks of him as legally elected, and as ruling in peace and prosperity. Thucydides seems to have used an Aleuad source, which was naturally pro-Athenian and anti-Daochid. The true state of affairs was that the anti-Athenian Daochus had been properly elected in 431 by a majority of the ruling class, and that later the resentment at the founding of Heraclêa had caused many to go over to the other party, so that Daochus, while still holding the archonship, was now the representative of a minority only. That there was in Thessaly a true democracy which befriended Athens, while the noble families were hostile to that city and on Sparta's side, is an untenable position.

§ 6. 1. Cf. Thuc. III 62 3; Aristot. Pol. IV 5 6–8 p. 1293a.
§ 6. 2. Homolle in BCH. XXI (1897) 592–598; cf. p. 9 supra.

Rejected - DO NOT FILM.
1984

Lightning Source UK Ltd.
Milton Keynes UK
07 February 2011

167064UK00005B/26/P